MW00778584

CLEANING

Lars Müller Publishers

Pleasant, somehow

気持ちいいのはなぜだろう。

舒适，缘何而来

舒適感、從何而來

기분 좋은 것은 어째서일까.

Armonia, dall'equilibrio

Irgendwie angenehm

L'harmonie, d'une certaine manière

Agradável, em equilíbrio

La armonía del equilibrio

L'harmonia de l'equilibri

Behagligt, på något sätt

Delvist behageligt

Sopivan mukavaa

Dễ chịu, theo cách nào đó

เหตุผลของความสบายใจ

السعادة، دون تكلف

sweep

掃く
打扫
清掃
쓸다
spazzare
fegen
balayer
varrer
barrer
escombrar
sopa
feje
lakaiseminen
quét dọn
כורד
كنس

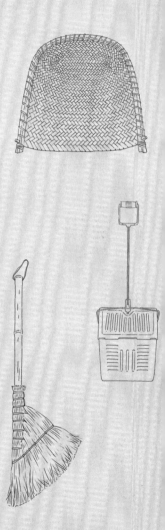

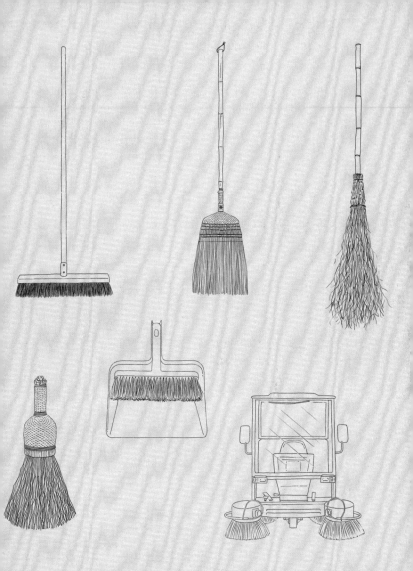

SWEEP

SWEEP

Sweeping the moss garden so as not to damage the moss
———— pp.008–013

SWEEP

SWEEP

Sweeping in front of a store
where there's heavy foot traffic

SWEEP

SWEEP

Vacuuming the theater carpet and wiping the seats
—— pp.016–019

SWEEP

Doing the daily vacuuming

SWEEP

Sweeping between the library stacks

SWEEP

SWEEP

Sweeping 399 steps, from top to bottom
——— pp.024–027

SWEEP

Sweeping the dust to the veranda along the lines of the tatami mats

SWEEP

Sweeping the street in the morning

SWEEP

Sweeping up before the guests arise is
part of the daily routine at this ryokan.
——— pp.032—035

SWEEP

SWEEP

Forgotten cleaning utensils

Tidying up after trimming the garden trees

SWEEP

SWEEP

Cleaning the mosque with a special carpet vacuum
———— pp.038–041

SWEEP

SWEEP

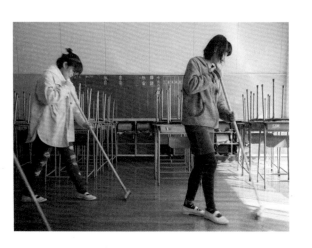

Elementary school classroom sweeping:
Begin by moving the desks and chairs to the side.
———— pp.042–045

SWEEP

SWEEP

Making a path in the park by sweeping away the fallen leaves

SWEEP

Sweeping in front of a bookstore in the bazaar

SWEEP

Monthly train cleaning

SWEEP

SWEEP

Sweeping the Great Wall of China —— pp.054–057

SWEEP

Sweeping the coop while chickens run to and fro

SWEEP

SWEEP

Sweeping under and between the concert hall seats

———— pp.060–063

SWEEP

SWEEP

SWEEP

The priest sweeps the church floor
in the setting afternoon sun.
———pp.066–071

SWEEP

SWEEP

Rising at 5 am, the monks begin cleaning the temple, sweeping before swabbing.

SWEEP

Sweeping up fallen leaves in front of the mosque

SWEEP

Sweeping away the dust that has
accumulated between the escalators

SWEEP

Sweeping the inner court of a traditional Siheyuan

SWEEP

Sweeping the streets of the hutong

SWEEP

Airport cleaning takes place quietly,
in the middle of the night.

SWEEP

A robot vacuum

SWEEP

SWEEP

Before the museum opens,
humans and robots clean together.

—— pp.086–089

SWEEP

A street sweeper

SWEEP

SWEEP

A truck with rotating brooms runs through the streets,
sweeping fallen leaves to the side.
—— pp.092–099

SWEEP

SWEEP

SWEEP

dust

払う
除尘
除塵
훑다
spazzolare
entstauben
épousseter
escovar
desempolvar
treure la pols
damma
afstøve
tomuttaminen
quét bụi
ฝุ่น
تنفيض

DUST

Dusting off the snow that
has accumulated on the lift

DUST

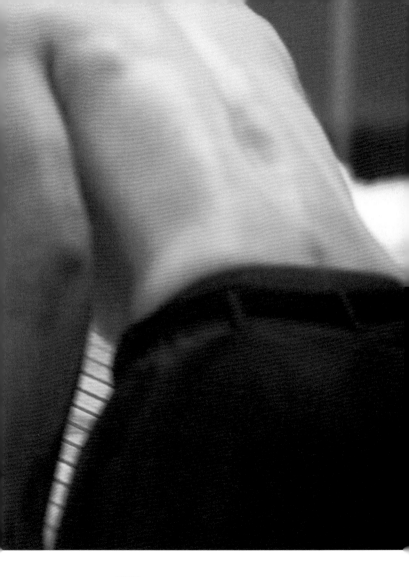

DUST

Cleaning up after the koji mold-making process at a sake brewery

——— pp.104–107

DUST

Dusting between the seats and backs of airport benches

Dusting the lint off of a suit before heading to work

DUST

Dusting lights at home

DUST

blow

吹き飛ばす

吹拭

吹拭

날려버리다

soffiare

wegblasen

souffler

soprar

limpiar soplando

netejar bufant

blåsa rent

blæse

puhtaaksi puhaltaminen

thổi sạch

เป่า

تنظيف بالهواء

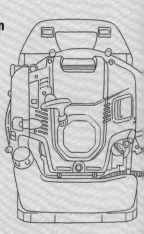

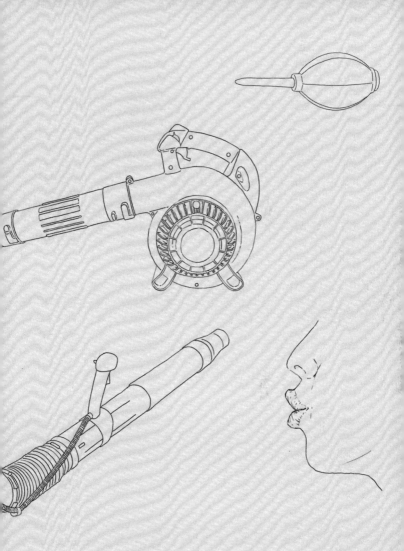

BLOW

BLOW

With the blowing away of fallen leaves, a vast lawn appears.

—— pp.114–117

BLOW

Blowing dust out of the spaces where fingers can't reach

BLOW

Carefully blowing and wiping dust from a camera lens

BLOW

BLOW

A maintenance worker blows away leaves in a park.
——— pp.122–125

BLOW

beat

はたく
捧除
拍拭
털다
spolverare
abstauben
sacudir
sacudir
frapper
batre
piska
banke
piiskaaminen
phủi bụi
ปัด
تنفيض الغبار

BEAT

BEAT

Every year on August 7, a ceremony known
as "Ominugui" is held at Japan's Todaiji Temple.
Going beyond cleaning the Great Buddha, it is a
discipline of the mind and body, a spiritual purification.

———— pp.128–135

BEAT

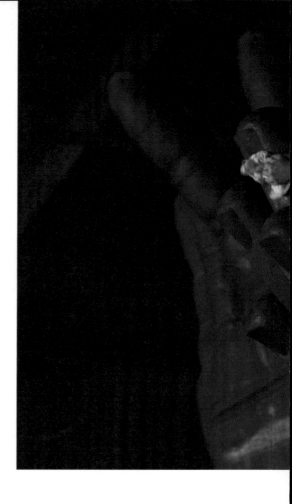

BEAT

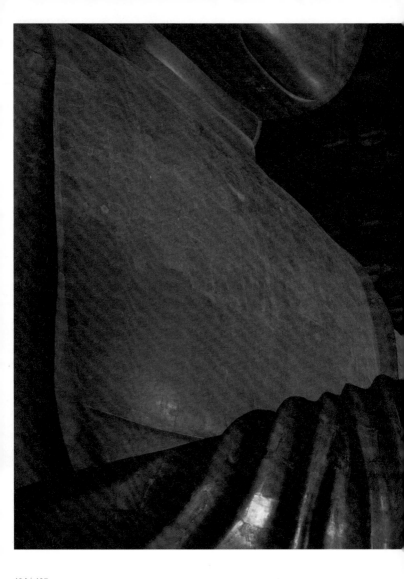

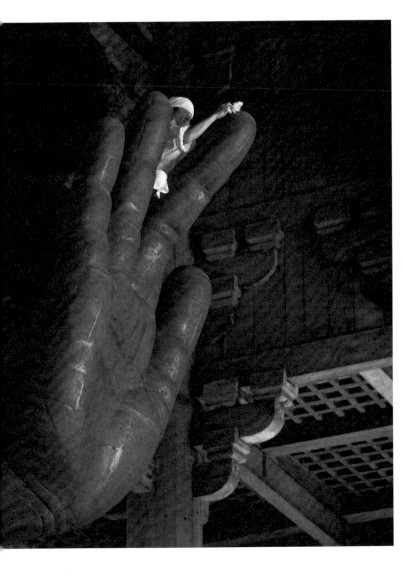

BEAT

An employee dusts a great stack of carpets.

BEAT

The homemade duster used in
this traditional Japanese restaurant
is made of washi paper.

BEAT

Dusting carefully so as not to rend the paper in these shoji doors

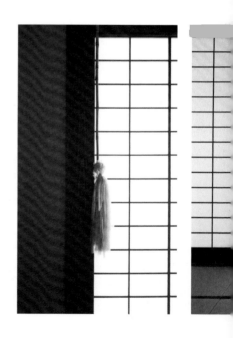

BEAT

Clapping chalkboard erasers together,
finishing with a small vacuum

BEAT

BEAT

Especially on a sunny day: airing the futons and beating them mightily
—— pp.144–147

BEAT

A duster hangs on the outer wall of a public restroom.

BEAT

—1

JAPAN'S BROOM VENDORS

Botefuri refers to the mobile street vendors
who once strode Japan's streets hawking their wares.
This peddler of traditional cleaning tools carries
bundles of brooms on both ends of his shoulder pole.
It's said that these vendors sold more than brooms:
Food, flowers and copper ware were among the variety of goods.

CLEANING

NATURAL SPONGE VENDORS IN GREECE

A peddler carrying his wares like a body suit sells
natural sponges on the street.
Natural sponges from the Mediterranean Sea,
both soft and high quality, have been used to clean
not only the body but also other surfaces
since the time of ancient Greece.

CLEANING TOOL
VENDORS IN THAILAND

Even today, mobile vendors carrying
masses of cleaning tools like brooms,
baskets, brushes and dusters tool through
residential neighborhoods of Thailand's cities on
bicycles or motorcycles modified for the purpose.
Their honking notifies potential customers.

* Illustration source: Photo by Richard Sharrocks/Moment/Getty Images

CLEANING

wash

洗う
清洗
清洗
씻다
lavare
waschen
laver
lavar
lavar
rentar
tvätta
vaske
peseminen
giặt rửa
ล้าง
غسل

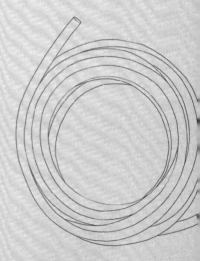

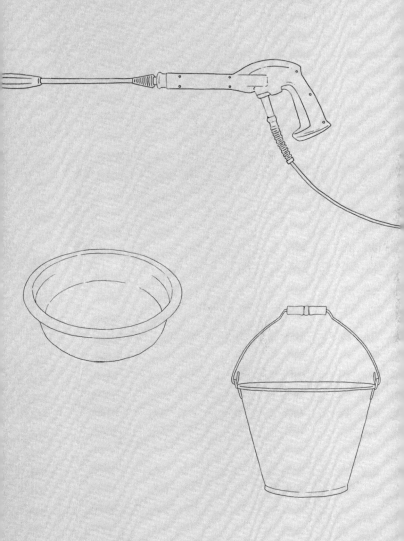

WASH

WASH

WASH

WASH

WASH

Nomads cleaning carpets in a valley
called "the gateway to heaven":
They gather all the village's carpets
and clean them all at once for Nowruz,
the Persian New Year,
which occurs on March 21st.
———pp.158–167

WASH

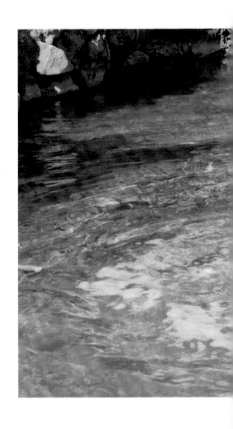

WASH

A public watering place where villagers wash carpets:
Some, feeling liberated as they clean, begin to swim.
—— pp.168–173

WASH

WASH

A father loads the dishwasher
after lunch with his family.

WASH

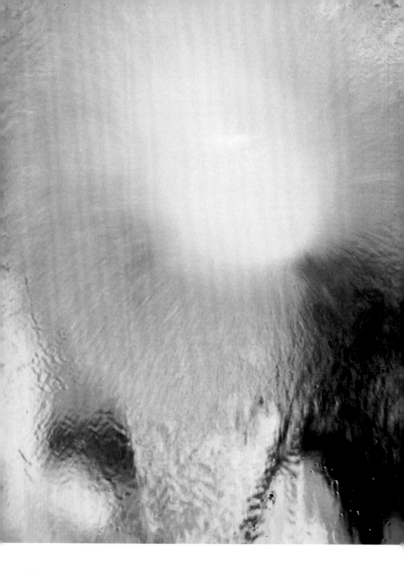

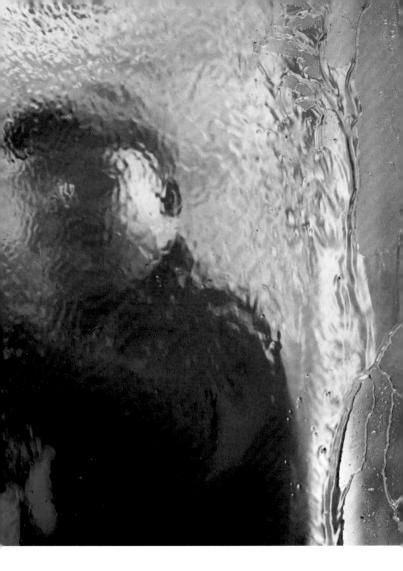

WASH

Deep cleaning the glass and exterior of a building
with a pressure washer
———— pp.176–179

WASH

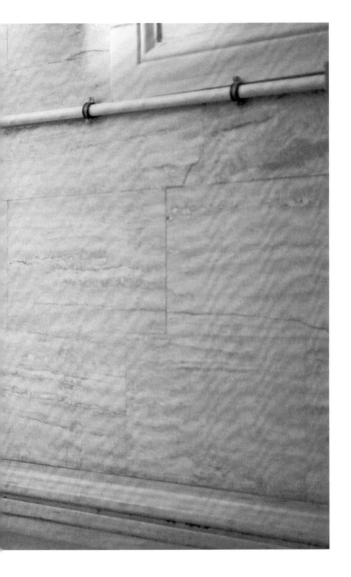

WASH

Cleaning the marble vestibule of a mosque

pp.180–183

WASH

So that guests can enjoy the sento comfortably on a daily basis, everything is cleaned carefully: baths, floors, basins, mirrors, etc.

———pp.184–187

WASH

WASH

Cleaning the corridor of a garden gazebo

WASH

Fish market cleaning is two-fold; washing down the floor rinses the fish.

WASH

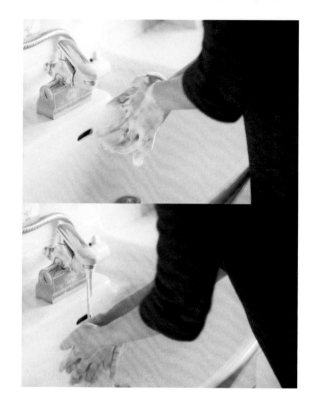

When you come home, wash your hands first.

After exercising in the schoolyard,
wash your hands and gargle.

WASH

Meticulous car washing, with affection

WASH

Cleaning a fixed shore trap net

WASH

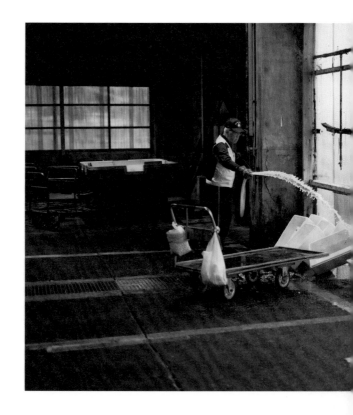

The auction at the port is over,
and empty fish boxes are washed out.

WASH

Shampooing dogs:
Wash a dog carefully with water
that's around 35 degrees Celcius.

WASH

WASH

A high-pressure cleaning system at the depot washes off the body of a slowly passing train. After stopping, the train is washed by hand.

pp.202–207

WASH

WASH

WASH

Cleaning a 150m-long ship from a large-scale dock
that is 260m long, 56.76m wide and 8.54m deep:
Shells and algae attached to the hull are rinsed off
with a power washer.

——— pp.208–217

WASH

WASH

WASH

WASH

WASH

Large passenger aircraft are cleaned late at night.
Planes are washed regularly on airport premises
not only to maintain aesthetics, but also to prevent a drop
in propulsion power due to accretion.
—— pp.218–223

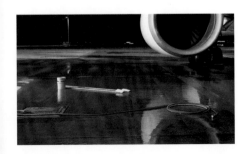

WASH

WASH

wipe

拭く
擦拭
擦拭
닦다
pulire
wischen
essuyer
limpar
limpiar
fregar
torka
aftørre
pyyhkiminen
lau chùi
เช็ด
مسح

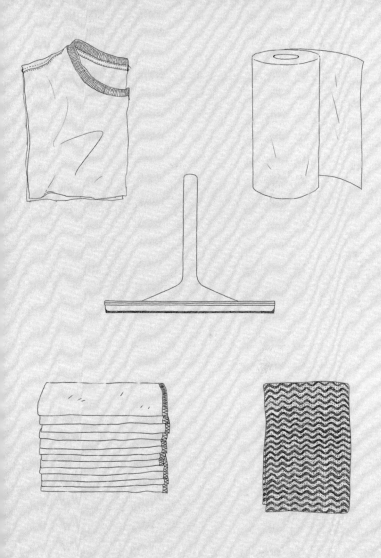

WIPE

Cleaning the exterior walls of a 43-story high rise:
Suspended by a single cable anchored to the roof,
workers in harnesses clean the windows.

—— pp.226–233

WIPE

WIPE

WIPE

Holding on to the frame and leaning out a bit,
the woman washes the window.
——— pp.234–237

WIPE

WIPE

Temple cleaning part two:
Monks first wipe tatami mats with damp cloths,
then wipe them dry, and also carefully wipe down the glass doors.
—— pp.238-241

WIPE

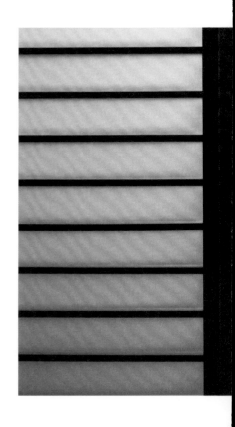

WIPE

This dining table has been wiped millions of times:
every morning, afternoon and evening.

WIPE

In a small shop, pottery is wiped meticulously
and carefully so as not to collide with other wares.

Gymnasium cleaning:
Students line up in a row and dry mop from one end to the other.

WIPE

The bookstore clerk wipes the dust off the spine of a book.

Tatami mats are wiped with a cotton cloth rinsed
with hot water and wrung out firmly.
Wooden handrails are wiped with a cloth soaked
in soapy water and wrung out lightly.

WIPE

Cleaning the elementary school classroom:
After sweeping, students wipe the floor with wet rags.

WIPE

Cleaning the elementary school corridor:
Students run in a single line while cleaning the floor with wet rags.

WIPE

aces of cleaning emerge in this full-length mirror as the sun sets.

WIPE

Creating a clear field of vision by wiping glasses clean

Wiping off the LCD after making a call

Walking through the theater aisles wiping down the backs of the seats one by one

WIPE

The violin is always wiped off after each session.
It's standard to dry it with a fine cloth.

WIPE

A symphony clarinetist cleans his instrument.
After the performance, it's a swift cleaning and a brisk return home.

WIPE

WIPE

Cleaning of the meditation hall starts early in the morning.
The wooden floors have been wiped down like this
for more than 350 years.
——— pp.266–271

WIPE

WIPE

WIPE

Church cleaning: The pastor wipes down the baptismal font,
the glass on the doors and the backs of the pews.

—— pp.272–275

WIPE

A sake brewer wipes the koji mold box clean.

WIPE

Wiping the train's hanging straps one by one with a glove-like cloth

WIPE

Wiping the glass flanking the escalator while descending

Using the escalator's motion to wipe down the handrails

WIPE

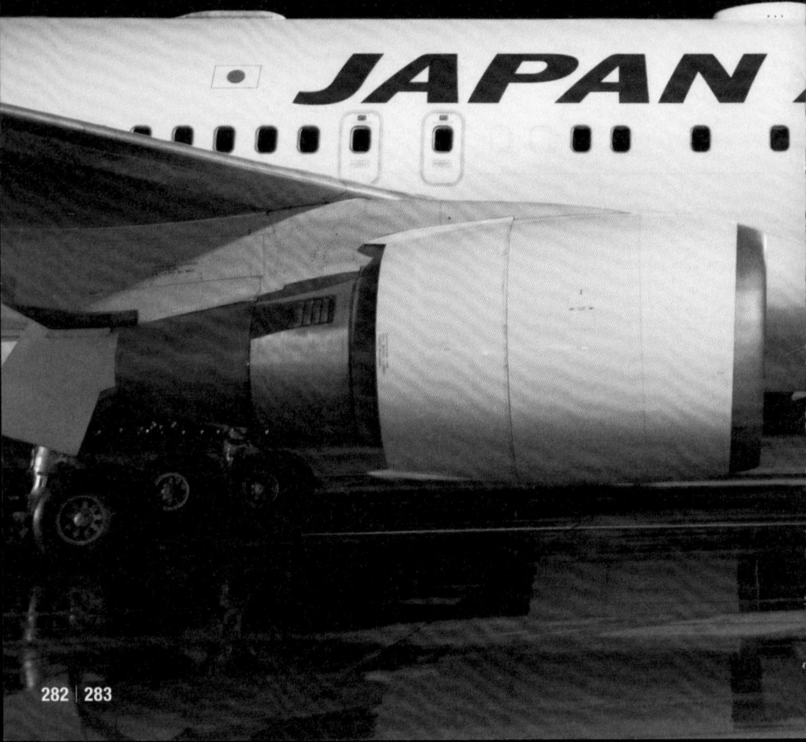
JAPAN

Cleaning bicycle wheels:
Grease stains the cloth black.

WIPE

A shop that sells miso by weight:
The shopkeeper wipes spilled miso off the counter.

At a seaside mackerel sandwich shop,
the grill is judiciously wiped clean with a paper towel
manipulated by a spatula.

WIPE

A bakery before dawn:
The glass facade is wiped down and the shop is ready to open.

WIPE

WIPE

Cleaning a giant aquarium with a maximum length of 34m,
a depth of 9m and a water volume of 5,400m³:
The divers wipe the acrylic resin panels from inside.

—— pp.290–293

WIPE

A highway on a rainy day:
Wipers swipe away the water.

WIPE

Extreme-scale cleaning

— **1**

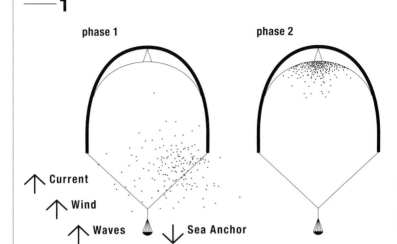

phase 1   phase 2

Current
Wind
Waves   Sea Anchor

GREAT PACIFIC
GARBAGE PATCH
CLEANUP*

* Information source: "The Ocean Cleanup"
  https://theoceancleanup.com/oceans/

phase 3

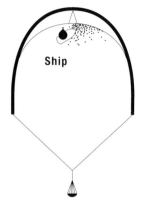

Ship

phase 4

The Ocean Cleanup is a marine debris
collection project conceived by then-high
school student Boyan Slat. The 600m-long
seine net system that collects drifting plastic
waste has been realized by combining the
natural forces of wind, sunlight, waves and
ocean currents with anchors, rather than
using energy derived from electricity or oil,
for example. The project aims to remove
half of The Great Pacific
Garbage Patch within five years.

1: A parachute anchor slows the
   movement of the seine system and,
   by maintaining a constant speed,
   allows fast-moving plastic waste to
   flow into the net.
2: Migrating through The Great Pacific
   Garbage Patch over an extended
   period of time, this system collects
   and temporarily retains the debris.
3: When full, the system is met by a ship.
4: The debris is collected by the visiting
   ship, and the system recirculates.

Extreme-scale cleaning

2

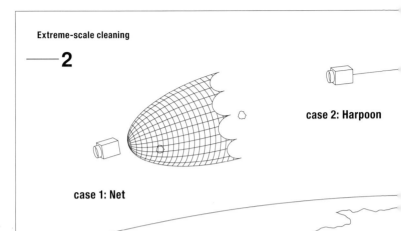

case 1: Net

case 2: Harpoon

SPACE DEBRIS
REMOVAL
—REMOVEDEBRIS*

* Information source: "Remove DEBRIS"
https://www.surrey.ac.uk/surrey-space-centre/missions/removedebris

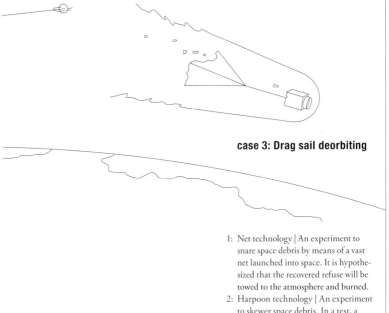

case 3: Drag sail deorbiting

Drifting in orbit around Earth, our home,
is a variety of space debris, including spent or
damaged satellites and rockets and wreckage
generated by explosions and collisions.
As space debris continues to accumulate hand
in hand with the progress of space exploration,
and is seen as a danger to astronauts and the
space station, a team led by the Surrey Space
Centre at the University of Surrey
has conducted three space debris cleanup
experiments in recent years.

1: Net technology | An experiment to
   snare space debris by means of a vast
   net launched into space. It is hypothe-
   sized that the recovered refuse will be
   towed to the atmosphere and burned.
2: Harpoon technology | An experiment
   to skewer space debris. In a test, a
   harpoon fired at a speed of 20m/sec
   successfully captured debris.
3: Drag sail deorbiting technology |
   Neither creating garbage nor cleaning
   it up, by means of a drag sail, a
   satellite that has reached the end of its
   operational life uses aerodynamic drag
   as a deorbiting force, carrying itself
   into the Earth's atmosphere to burn
   itself up. This measure aims not to
   reduce space debris by cleaning it up,
   but rather to not increase debris
   in the first place.

CLEANING

ORGANIZATION AND CLEANING ARE RELATED

From the Japanese term *seiriseiton*, which roughly translates as "organization and orderliness," we tend to think that the activity of neatly organizing things leads to orderliness, but even when a desk is strewn with documents and books, as in the cases of those of magazine and newspaper editors, it's likely that the person using the desk can easily locate any and all necessary information. In other words, even if an outsider might describe this as a chaotic information environment, to the person in question, it is organized. Because the definition of "organization" is so individually nuanced, indexing is an effective means of sharing information with others. An indicator becomes a trail, a clue, a handhold, by which people can share the whereabouts of information and the tracks followed by those who came before. Although the act of attaching an indicator, such as a label or sticky note, takes a little extra effort, it can be considered a small act of cleaning, giving long life to groups of information that if neglected, would surely have been buried in obscurity.

smooth

ならす

整平

整平

고르게 하다

uniformare

glätten

lisser

alisar

alisar

allisar

jämna ut

udglatte

siloittaminen

làm nhẵn

ปรับเรียบ

تمليس

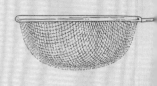

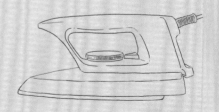

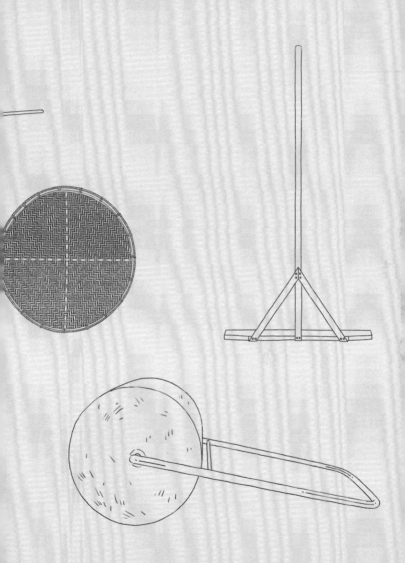

SMOOTH

SMOOTH

On a post-game hockey rink, the ice is uneven.
A resurfacer shaves off a thin top layer of ice and sprays water as it goes.
The spray freezes, creating a smooth surface.

—— pp.304–307

SMOOTH

"Dragonfly rakes" stand ready to level soil and sand on the athletic fields.

SMOOTH

Ironing to smooth out the wrinkles

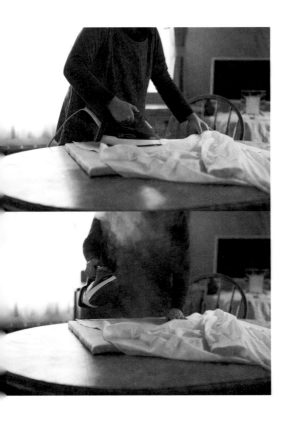

SMOOTH

SMOOTH

After scooping, the storekeeper smooths the spices
into gentle curves with spatula and scoop.
——— pp.312–315

SMOOTH

Leveling the ash in a sunken hearth with a broom

SMOOTH

Sifting the ash into a fine powder
and spreading it in the hearth

Before the concert starts:
smoothing the footprints out of the carpet's nap
to welcome the audience

SMOOTH

rake

かく

耙扫

耙掃

긁어내다

rastrellare

rechen

ratisser

juntar

rastrillar

rastellar

kratta

rive

haravoiminen

cào

คราด

تسوية

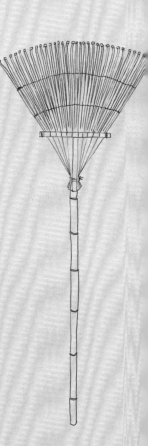

RAKE

RAKE

Patterns in the gravel, disturbed by pedestrians,
are recreated with a rake-like iron tool.
———pp.324–327

RAKE

groom

ととのえる

整理

修整

정돈하다

spuntare

zurechtmachen

tailler

arranjar

arreglar

polir

vårda

rengøre

siistiminen

chải

ตัดแต่ง

ترتيب

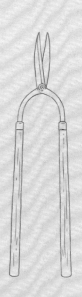

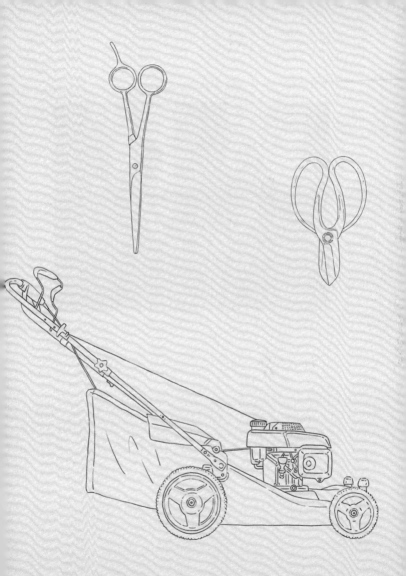

GROOM

Once the guests have left the room,
hotel staff clean up, changing sheets,
preparing beds and replenishing amenities.

GROOM

Personal grooming starts with hairstyling.

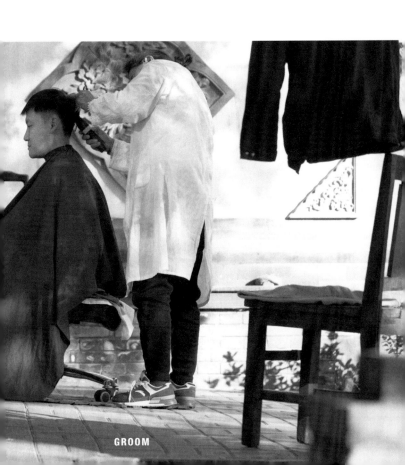

GROOM

Bonsai pruning

GROOM

Tending vines entangled in the chain link fence
that serves as a privacy screen

Mowing the lawn and maintaining the garden

GROOM

Trimming the hedge with pruners

GROOM

GROOM

Pre-performance grooming:
Straw is removed from the whole body of the supine elephant.
———— pp.340–343

GROOM

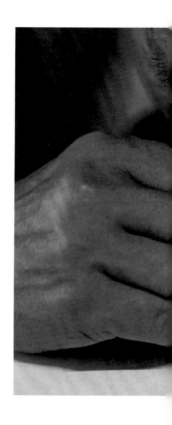

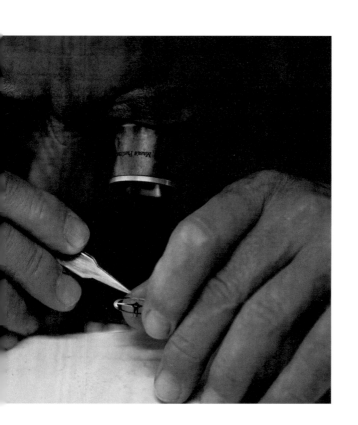

GROOM

The overhaul of clocks and watches that includes dismantling
and cleaning the inside, injecting new machine oil and reassembly
is the mechanical version of a complete medical checkup.

—— pp.344–349

GROOM

GROOM

purify

清める

清理

淨化

정결히 하다

purificare

reinigen

purifier

purificar

purificar

purificar

rena

rense

puhdistaminen

làm sạch

ชำระ

تنقية

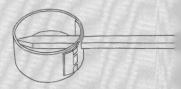

PURIFY

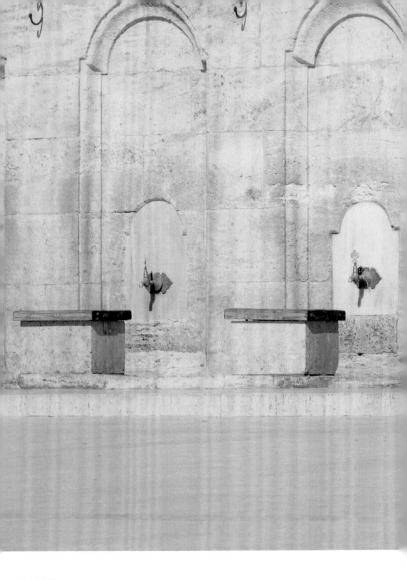

PURIFY

Prior to praying, worshipers perform a purifying ritual
by washing parts of their body with water outside the mosque.
——— pp.352–355

PURIFY

People perform a ritual cleansing
at the chozusha (water ablution pavilion)
before paying homage at a shrine or temple.

PURIFY

PURIFY

Oharai is a purification ritual.

PURIFY

scrub

磨く

打磨

磨拭

윤을 내다

strofinare

schrubben

astiquer

esfregar

restregar

friccionar

skrubba

skrubbe

hankaaminen

cọ rửa

ขัด

تنظيف بالفرك

SCRUB

SCRUB

The crew polishes the deck of the ship with coconut cross sections.
Sprinkling seawater on the deck, they squat side by side, and shout as they polish.
This job is called "turn to" (as in turn to the work).
——— pp.364–369

SCRUB

SCRUB

Drip a little soap on the cloth, and polish the counter.

SCRUB

SCRUB

Before the early summer opening, the lazy river pool is cleaned.
———— pp.372–377

SCRUB

SCRUB

Cleaning the griddle at an okonomiyaki restaurant:
The inlaid iron griddle must be cleaned
while it's hot to ensure that food remains and blemishes
are removed, helping to extend its useful life.

SCRUB

To make sure the kitchen can be used for a long time,
after cooking, the area around the burners and the grout
between the tiles are cleaned and polished well,
and all grease is completely removed.

SCRUB

Polishing the pothook that hangs over
the sunken hearth

Various tools for cleaning the airport floors

Polishing his daily commuting buddy

SCRUB

In his black hat and black clothes,
the chimneysweep carries his circular wire brush on his back.
In Germany, the chimneysweep is considered a bearer of good luck.

—— pp.386–389

SCRUB

SCRUB

Military shoe polish: Basically, a single set includes three kinds of brushes:
one for removing dirt, one for applying cream to the leather,
and one to brush away excess cream for a shiny finish.

——— pp.390–393

SCRUB

Polishing a hot spring's stone bath: The sound echoes.

SCRUB

The shoeshine: He carries a footrest
in which are stored both brushes and wax.
——— pp.396–399

SCRUB

SCRUB

scrape

剥がす

剥除

剝除

떼다

raschiare

ablösen

gratter

raspar

raspar

raspar

skrapa

skrabe

raaputtaminen

nạo vét

ขูด

كشط

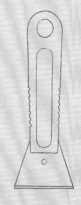

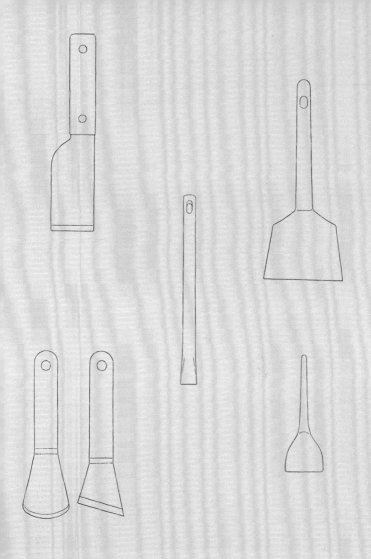

SCRAPE

SCRAPE

Peeling stickers from a road sign
——— pp.402–405

SCRAPE

BROOM

On a broom shaped like a large brush
or fude (ink brush), the bristles curl and bend,
becoming distorted with continued handling.
With repetition, the shape of the tool reflects
the sweeping motion of the user.
The bristles show changes unique to each user,
inconceivable when the product is new
and beyond the imagination of its manufacturer.
Despite such unexpected metamorphosis
in our oft-used tools,
we simply continue to use them
as we grow more attached.

SPONGE

Dishwashing: scraping off oil and debris stuck
on dishes as detergent aids with dissolution.
Since delicate human skin cannot withstand
the frequent dishwashing that is part of day-to-day cleaning,
sponges have come into widespread use.
Subject not only to the wear and tear of daily use,
but also to the effects of ultraviolet rays, heat, hydrolysis
and detergents, even the flexible sponge transforms over time.

CLEANING

—— 3

SHOE BRUSH

Brushes remove dust and dirt
through the friction of fine bristles over uneven surfaces.
With use, the bristles spread, soften and change color.
This discoloration is caused by the accumulated oil
from creams and waxes, not by deterioration.
By polishing shoes with a brush with bristles so discolored,
oil is transferred to the leather, restoring luster.

erase

消す
消除
消除
지우다
cancellare
löschen
effacer
apagar
borrar
esborrar
ta bort
slette
eliminoiminen
loại bỏ
au
إزالة

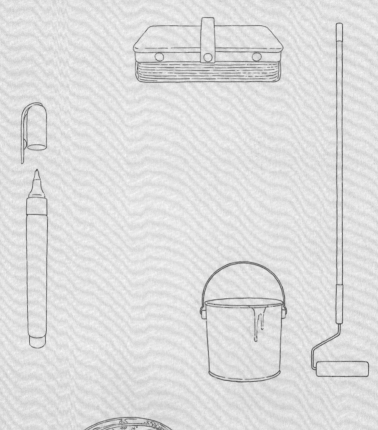

ERASE

Erasing mistakes in the ledger

ERASE

After class, erasing the chalk from the board

ERASE

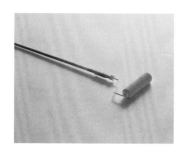

A photo studio: Because even the slightest blemish
becomes "noise" in a photograph,
the white background is repainted regularly.

ERASE

Repainting a hotel's porte-cochère

ERASE

Shredding unneccessary documents

ERASE

scoop

すくう

撈除

撈除

떠내다

raccogliere

aufnehmen

ramasser

recolher

recoger

agafar

skopa

skovle

kauhominen

vớt

ตัก

تنظيف بالمجرفة

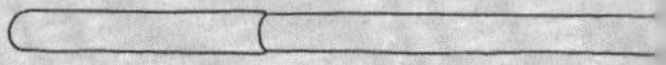

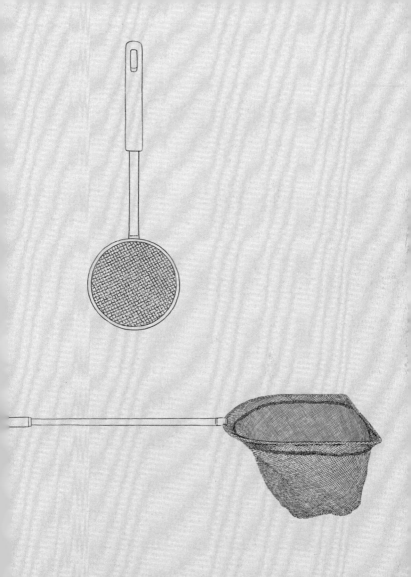

SCOOP

SCOOP

Scooping algae from a pond:
If it's unreachable from shore, go by boat.
——— pp.426–429

SCOOP

Scooping up tenkasu:
what's left over after frying tempura

remove

除く
清除
清除
치우다
togliere
entfernen
ôter
remover
quitar
treure
avlägsna
fjerne
poistaminen
thải bỏ
ขจัด
إزالة

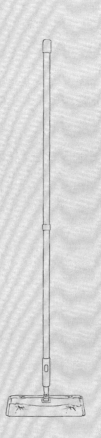

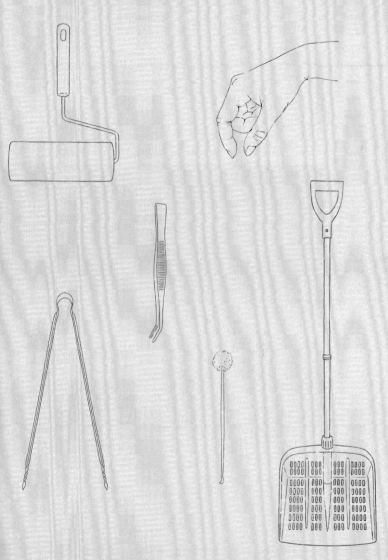

REMOVE

Removing fallen leaves from an open air bath

REMOVE

REMOVE

Snow is removed, first by shovel, and then by snowplow.

—— pp.436–439

REMOVE

A couple shoveling snow in front of their house:
Two working together finish more quickly than one working alone.

REMOVE

REMOVE

Removing excrement and other debris that blankets the sand on
the bottom of the aquarium is vital to maintain water quality and stability.
——— pp.442–445

REMOVE

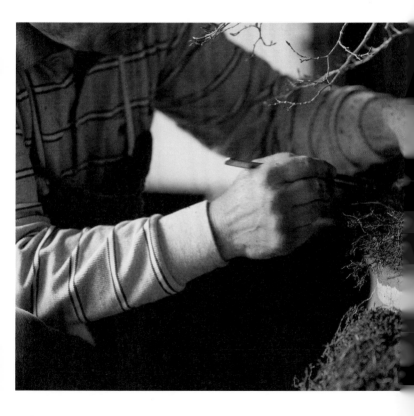

Bonsai replanting: A bonsai tree must be regularly repotted.
Because overgrown roots begin to choke off the air supply,
the plant must be removed from its container,
its unnecessary roots trimmed, and old soil removed from the roots.

REMOVE

The chiritori process in washi paper making:
Under running water, stray particles and bits of bark that have become mixed with
the fibers are painstakingly plucked out by hand.

REMOVE

After this, a careful eye is turned to any remaining foreign objects, and these are removed by hand.

REMOVE

In the absence of a strike or a spare,
the remaining pins are removed and set up for the next frame.

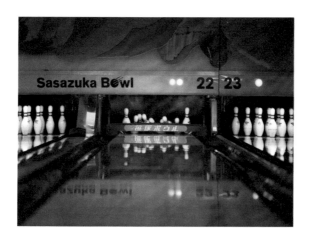

REMOVE

clear

片付ける

収拾

收拾

정리하다

ripulire

aufräumen

ranger

eliminar

despejar

recollir

städa undan

rydde

tyhjentäminen

thu dọn

กำจัดออก

جمع المخلفات

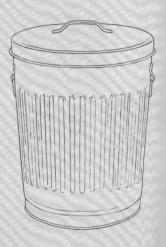

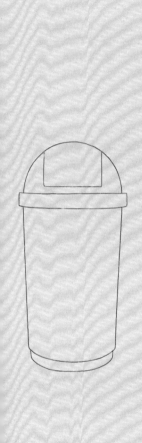

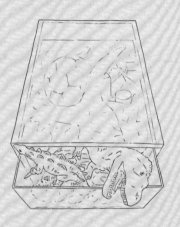

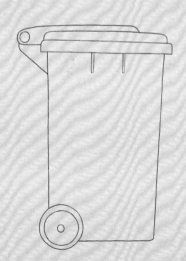

CLEAR

As worshippers are called to prayer, the remains of a chat over chai in a corner of the mosque are cleared away.

CLEAR

Cleaning up the toys

CLEAR

Public garbage cans with ashtrays are equipped with
mechanisms displaying the amount of trash accumulated within.

CLEAR

Restaurant tidying after customers exit:
Carrying away dishes and wiping tables clean

CLEAR

Collecting garbage bags from the receptacles in a public park

CLEAR

A leaf vacuum that also functions as a lawn mower traverses the grounds of a vast public park.

CLEAR

Folding futons and storing them in the closet

CLEAR

CLEAR

A garbage collection center in the city:
People bring in their household garbage by car,
and dispose of it in designated compartments.
When this overflows, it is compressed with a machine.

—— pp.470–473

CLEAR

A garbage collection center gathers a variety of waste,
from large electronic appliances to small items such as disks
and light bulbs. What can be recycled is repurposed as new resources.
—— pp.474–477

CLEAR

Trash in the trash bin, properly

CLEAR

From the trash bin to the industrial waste treatment plant.
Instead of incinerating it, we thoroughly sort and classify waste
by whatever process is available, including human hands, machines, AI, wind
and magnetism. This is the work we must do in order to
reduce the amount of waste and to recycle it as a resource.

CLEAR

CLEAR

Pleasant, somehow

We call environments that people have created in response to nature "man-made." That which is man-made should be comfortable, but when materials that encroach upon or erode nature, like plastic and concrete, become widespread, people begin to yearn for nature. And yet, when nature is left to its own devices, dust and fallen leaves pile up, and plants thrive wildly. As a result, historically, human beings have lived by accepting nature to a certain extent and also keeping it moderately in check. And so, in creating a residence or a garden, it's uncouth and tasteless to allow the man-made to predominate. We must allow nature a moderate reign, neither over-sweeping the fallen leaves nor over-pruning the greenery. Just as at the water's edge, where the breaking waves cleanse the sandy beach, the ultimate secret of cleaning may be found where human agency and nature struggle against one another, in our pursuit of "moderate comfort."

In 2019, we went around the world photographing scenes in which people were pictured cleaning. This was before COVID-19 swept the globe. We had been wondering if the very essence of human beings lies dormant in the everyday and ordinary work of cleaning, which transcends culture and civilization. When the entire world stopped, these photos and videos made us miss our ordinary routines. No matter how technology advances in the future, people are living things, embracing a rhythm of life that perpetually resonates in the depth of the body. We can move forward heeding this natural internal rhythm.

気持ちいいのは
なぜだろう。

自然に対してヒトがなした環境を「人工」といいます。人工は心地がいいはずなのですが、プラスチックやコンクリートのように自然を侵食する素材が蔓延してくると、ヒトは自然を恋しがるようになります。しかし自然は、放っておくと埃や落ち葉が降り積もり、草木は奔放に生い茂ります。したがって、自然をほどほどに受け入れつつ、適度に排除しながらヒトは暮らしてきたのでしょう。家や庭をつくるにも、人工が勝りすぎるのは野暮。落ち葉は掃きすぎず、草木も刈りすぎず程よく茂るに任せます。まるで、打ち寄せる波が砂浜をあらう渚のように、人為と自然がせめぎ合う「ほどほどの心地よさ」を探し当てること、それが「掃除」の極意なのかもしれません。

2019年、私たちは世界中の掃除のシーンを撮影しました。COVID-19が世界を席巻する前のことです。文化や文明を超えて営まれる掃除というごく普通の営みの中に、ヒトの本質が潜んでいるのではないかと考えてのことでした。世界が止まってしまったあの時、その写真や映像を見直すと、ごくあたり前の暮らしがとてもいとおしく感じられました。この先の未来においてどんなに技術が進んでも、ヒトは生き物。身体の奥底に響き続ける生のリズムがあります。ここに耳をすませていきたいものです。

CLEANING

舒适，缘何而来

相对自然，人创造的环境称为"人工"。人工，会令人心感舒适，但当塑料或混凝土等侵蚀自然的人工材料不断蔓延，人又反过来开始怀恋自然。而如果放任"自然"，那么就会任由尘埃枯叶落积，草木野蛮生长。因此人对自然，是在不断适当地接受，同时又适度排除的过程中一路走来的。建造房屋和庭园亦然。过分凸显人工，便会背离自然。落叶，不必清扫得太过干净；草木，也无需割除殆尽，不妨适度任其生长。宛如涌上沙滩的波浪退去后留下的洲渚，也许探寻人为与自然在相生相克中达成的"适度舒适"才是"扫除"的真谛。

2019年，我们拍摄了世界各地的扫除场景。那时，新冠疫情尚未席卷全球。当时曾想：超越文化与文明又极其普通的日常扫除活动中，是否潜藏着人的本质。如今世界停摆，此时重新看看那些照片和影像，不由感慨：平凡的生活竟是如此美好。放眼未来，无论技术如何进步，人还是自然界的生物。人的身体发肤始终回响着生生不息的节律，令人想侧耳聆听。

舒適感、從何而來

相對於自然，人所創造出來的環境稱為「人工」。人工是為了讓人過得更舒適，但是在塑膠及水泥等素材過分使用而侵蝕自然之後，人類又回頭開始盼望能回歸自然。然而，若放任自然不做約束，則塵埃與落葉將會堆積如山，草木也會恣意奔放生長。所以，適度接受自然，適度加入人工，就是身為人類的我們一直以來的生活模式。建造房屋及庭院時，過分突顯人工，就會背離自然。清潔的時候，也許可以留下幾片落葉，讓草木自由生長而不過度修剪。就如同海浪沖刷後留下的沙灘波紋一般，探究尋找人與自然在共生共存中所平衡的「適度舒適感」，才是「清潔」的真諦。

當新型冠狀病毒（COVID-19）尚未席捲世界之前，在2019年，我們拍攝了世界各地的清潔場景。我們認為，看似普遍的日常清潔活動中，或許潛藏著超越文明與文化的人類本質。如今，當世界因新型冠狀病毒而停擺，我們重新觀看這些照片與影像，不禁懷念起那些日常的美好。放眼未來，無論科技如何演進，人類始終是生物。只要我們側耳傾聽，就會發現那存在於身體深處的原始律動

기분 좋은 것은
어째서일까.

자연에 맞서 사람이 만들어낸 환경을 '인공' 이라 합니다. 그렇기에 인공은 편안할 터입니다. 하지만 인간은 플라스틱과 콘크리트처럼 자연을 지나치게 침식하는 소재가 주변에 만연하면 자연을 다시 갈망합니다. 자연 또한 내버려 두면 먼지와 낙엽이 쌓이고 풀과 나무가 무성해집니다. 그래서 사람들은 자연을 어느 정도 받아들이고, 또 어느 정도 배제하며 삶을 이어왔습니다. 이건 집과 정원을 만들 때도 마찬가지라, 인공적인 티가 너무 많이 나면 멋없어지기 마련입니다. 떨어진 잎사귀를 전부 쓸어내고 풀과 나무를 요란하게 다듬는 대신, 적당히 내버려 두는 건 어떨까요. 파도가 모래사장을 쓸어내는 바닷가처럼 인간과 자연 사이에 존재하는 '적당한 편안함' 을 찾아 균형을 맞추는 것. 그것이 '청소' 가 가진 진정한 의미일지도 모르겠네요. 2019년, 우리는 전 세계를 다니며 청소하는 모습을 촬영했습니다. COVID-19가 전 세계에 퍼지기 전입니다. 문명과 문화권을 뛰어넘어 이루어지는 이 청소라는 평범한 행위 속에, 사람의 본질이 숨어 있지는 않을까 하는 생각에서였습니다. 세계가 멈춰 버린 지금, 그 사진과 영상을 다시 보니 지극히 당연했던 생활이 너무나 그립게만 느껴집니다. 앞으로 기술이 아무리 발전한다 해도, 인간이 살아있는 생명체임은 변하지 않을 것입니다. 몸 깊숙한 곳에서 생명의 리듬이 울려 퍼지고 있습니다. 우리는 이 소리에 귀를 기울이며 앞으로 나아가고자 합니다.

Armonia,
dall'equilibrio

Gli ambienti creati dall'uomo, che si contrappongono a quelli naturali, sono detti "artificiali". Ciò che è artificiale deve essere confortevole, ma quando vi è una proliferazione di materiali che alterano troppo la natura, come la plastica e il cemento, iniziamo a rimpiangere ciò che è naturale. D'altro canto, se non interveniamo in alcun modo sulla natura, la polvere e le foglie cadute si accumulano e la vegetazione prospera in modo selvaggio. Questo è probabilmente il motivo per cui gli esseri umani vivono in parte accettando e in parte abbattendo la natura. Analogamente, anche quando si creano abitazioni o giardini, l'artificialità non è mai predominante, al fine di evitare un effetto finale rozzo e inelegante. Lascia libera la natura almeno in parte, non rastrellare fino all'ultima foglia e non potare eccessivamente il verde. Come nella battigia, dove le onde si infrangono lambendo la sabbia, il segreto del pulire è appunto la ricerca di un "comfort moderato", in cui l'azione dell'uomo e la forza della natura si scontrano e si incontrano.

Nel 2019 abbiamo fotografato in giro per il mondo persone ritratte nell'atto del pulire. Prima che il COVID-19 si diffondesse ovunque. Ci chiedevamo se la vera essenza degli esseri umani non risiedesse latente proprio nell'atto quotidiano e ordinario del pulire, comune a ogni cultura e civiltà. Quando il mondo intero si è fermato, riguardando quelle foto e quei video abbiamo scoperto di avere nostalgia di quei gesti consueti. Nonostante i progressi tecnologici, l'essenza umana si fonde con la natura seguendo un ritmo vitale che si perpetua incessantemente. Possiamo superare questo momento ascoltando proprio quel ritmo interno naturale.

Irgendwie angenehm

Umgebungen, die wir Menschen als Abgrenzung zur Natur geschaffen haben, nennen wir «menschengemacht». Alles Künstliche, Menschengemachte soll bequem sein. Aber wenn die dafür verwendeten Materialien zu sehr in die Natur eingreifen oder sie sogar zurückdrängen, wie bei Kunststoff und Beton, beginnen die Menschen, sich nach der Natur zu sehnen. Überlässt man jedoch die Natur sich selbst, häufen sich Staub und Laub an, und Pflanzen nehmen überhand. So kam es, dass die Menschen historisch gesehen die Natur bis zu einem gewissen Grad akzeptierten und sie dabei moderat bändigten. Gestaltet man daher eine Wohnung oder einen Garten, wirkt es unkultiviert und geschmacklos, wenn das Menschengemachte dominiert. Wir müssen der Natur eine angemessene Herrschaft erlauben, also weder das Laub zu sauber wegfegen noch das Grün zu stark beschneiden. So wie am Meeresufer, wo die brechenden Wellen den Sandstrand waschen, mag sich die Antwort auf das Geheimnis des Ordnung-Schaffens an Orten verbergen, an denen sich Natur und Mensch aneinander reiben, auf unserer Suche nach gemäßigtem Komfort.

2019 bereisten wir die Welt und fotografierten Menschen beim Reinigen. Das war zu einer Zeit bevor COVID-19 um den Globus «fegte». Wir hatten uns gefragt, ob das Wesen des Menschen vielleicht in unseren alltäglichen und ganz normalen Reinigungsarbeiten schlummert, die Kulturen und Zivilisationen übergreifend existieren. Als die ganze Welt stehen geblieben schien, liessen uns diese Fotos und Videos unsere gewöhnlichen Routinen vermissen. Unabhängig davon, wie die Technologie in Zukunft voranschreitet, sind Menschen Lebewesen, die einen Lebensrhythmus anstreben, der in der Tiefe ihrer Seele resoniert. Wenn wir diesem natürlichen inneren Rhythmus Gehör schenken, können wir voranschreiten.

L'harmonie,
d'une certaine manière

Les espaces créés par les humains pour faire face à la nature sont appelés ouvrages humains. Ces espaces sont destinés à être confortables, mais lorsque des matériaux qui rongent la nature ou la mettent en péril, comme les plastiques et le béton, deviennent trop répandus, les humains aspirent à davantage de nature. D'un autre côté, lorsque la nature est laissée libre de se développer, la poussière et les feuilles mortes s'amoncellent, et les plantes sauvages deviennent envahissantes. C'est pour cette raison que, dans l'histoire, les êtres humains ont vécu en acceptant la nature jusqu'à un certain point tout en la gardant sous contrôle de façon modérée. Lors de la construction d'une maison ou de la création d'un jardin, il est considéré comme indélicat et comme un manque de goût que l'ouvrage humain prenne le dessus sur la nature. Nous devons laisser à la nature des espaces de liberté sans balayer trop systématiquement les feuilles mortes ni tailler à l'excès les végétaux. Tels les rivages où les vagues nettoient les plages de sable, le secret ultime du nettoyage réside peut-être là où l'activité humaine lutte à armes égales avec la nature à la recherche d'un confort équilibré.

En 2019, nous avons parcouru le monde afin de photographier des personnes en train de nettoyer. Nous avons fait cela avant que le COVID-19 n'ébranle le monde. Nous cherchions à savoir si l'essence même des êtres humains résidait dans les tâches de nettoyage quotidiennes et ordinaires, qui transcendent les cultures et civilisations. Lorsque le monde entier s'est arrêté, ces photos et ces vidéos nous ont rappelés à quel point ces activités qui font notre quotidien nous manquaient. Quelles que soient les avancées technologiques dont nous serons témoins dans le futur, les humains resteront des êtres vivants embrassant le rythme de la vie qui résonne de façon constante au plus profond de leurs corps. Nous pouvons aller de l'avant en restant à l'écoute de ce rythme naturel présent en chacun de nous.

Agradável, em equilíbrio

Chamamos "artificiais" aos ambientes que as pessoas criaram como resposta à natureza. O que é artificial deve ser confortável, mas quando os materiais que invadem ou desgastam a natureza, tais como o plástico e o betão, se tornam generalizados, as pessoas começam a ansiar pela natureza. Porém, quando a natureza fica entregue a si própria, o pó e as folhas caídas acumulam-se e as plantas crescem de forma selvagem. Como consequência, historicamente, os seres humanos têm vivido, aceitando a natureza até certa medida e mantendo-a moderadamente sob controlo. Assim, ao construir uma casa ou um jardim, é considerado grosseiro e falta de gosto permitir que o artificial predomine. Devemos conceder à natureza um domínio moderado, não devemos varrer as folhas caídas em demasia nem podar excessivamente a vegetação. Tal como à beira-mar, onde a rebentação das ondas varre a areia da praia, o derradeiro segredo da limpeza pode ser encontrado onde a ação humana e a natureza lutam entre si, na nossa busca de um "conforto moderado".

Em 2019, viajámos pelo mundo e fotografámos momentos em que as pessoas estavam a limpar. Isto foi antes de o COVID-19 se espalhar pelo mundo. Perguntámos a nós mesmos se a verdadeira essência do ser humano se encontra latente nas tarefas de limpeza comuns do dia a dia, que transcendem a cultura e a civilização. Quando o mundo inteiro parou, estes vídeos e fotografias fizeramos com que sintamos falta das nossas rotinas diárias. Independentemente de como a tecnologia evoluirá no futuro, as pessoas são seres vivos e abraçam um ritmo de vida que ressoa perpetuamente no âmago do seu corpo. Podemos seguir em frente, prestando atenção a este ritmo interno natural.

La armonía del equilibrio

Los entornos que hemos creado en respuesta a la naturaleza los llamamos "artificiales". Lo artificial debe ser cómodo, pero cuando proliferan materiales que son invasivos o destructivos para la naturaleza, como el plástico o el hormigón, la gente comienza a echar en falta la naturaleza. Sin embargo, cuando dejamos que la naturaleza siga su curso con toda libertad, el polvo y las hojas caídas se acumulan, y las plantas crecen incontroladamente. Como resultado, históricamente, los seres humanos hemos vivido aceptando la naturaleza hasta cierto punto, y a la vez manteniéndola moderadamente bajo control. Y, por lo tanto, al crear una vivienda o un jardín, está mal visto si se permite que predomine lo artificial. Debemos dejar que la naturaleza mantenga un moderado dominio: sin barrer completamente todas las hojas caídas, ni cortar excesivamente la vegetación. Al igual que en la orilla del mar, donde las olas rompen y bañan las playas de arena, el secreto de la limpieza se encuentra quizás en descubrir un equilibrio en el que la actividad humana y la naturaleza se enfrenten entre ellas, en nuestro intento por alcanzar una "comodidad moderada".

En 2019, fuimos por todo el mundo fotografiando escenas en las que la gente aparecía haciendo limpieza. Esto fue antes de que COVID-19 asolara el mundo. Y hemos estado preguntándonos si la esencia misma de los seres humanos no se encuentra de forma latente en la labor diaria y común de la limpieza, algo que trasciende culturas y civilizaciones. Cuando el mundo entero se detuvo, estas fotos y vídeos nos hicieron añorar nuestras rutinas cotidianas. Por mucho que la tecnología avance en el futuro, las personas somos seres vivos, y adoptamos un ritmo de vida que resuena perpetuamente en lo más profundo de nuestros organismos. Podemos seguir avanzando hacia adelante, dejándonos guiar por este ritmo interno natural.

L'harmonia de l'equilibri

Dels entorns que les persones han creat en resposta a la naturalesa en diem "artificials". Les coses artificials haurien de ser còmodes, però quan s'estenen els materials que afecten o erosionen la natura, com el plàstic i el formigó, la gent la comença a enyorar. Tot i així, quan es deixa que la naturalesa segueixi el seu curs natural, la pols i les fulles caigudes s'acumulen i les plantes creixen sense límits. Com a resultat d'això, històricament l'ésser humà ha viscut acceptant la natura fins a cert punt i al mateix temps mantenint-la mitjanament controlada. D'aquesta manera, quan es crea un lloc per viure o un jardí, està mal vist que hi predomini l'artificialitat. Hem de cedir a la naturalesa un cert domini: ni escombrar les fulles caigudes ni reduir-ne la vegetació. Com passa a la vora del mar, on les onades trenquen i banyen la platja de sorra, el secret de la neteja rau en descobrir un equilibri allà on l'ésser humà i la naturalesa xoquen, en un intent d'assolir la "comoditat moderada".

El 2019 vam fer la volta al món fotografiant escenes de persones netejant. Això va ser abans que la COVID-19 causés un gran impacte al planeta. Ens hem preguntat si la pròpia essència de l'ésser humà rau en el treball quotidià i ordinari de neteja, que va més enllà de la cultura i la civilització. Avui en dia, que el món sencer s'ha aturat, aquestes fotografies i vídeos ens fan enyorar les rutines habituals. Per més que la tecnologia avanci en el futur, les persones són éssers vius enganxades un ritme de vida que ressona en la profunditat del cos de manera indefinida. Podem avançar atenent aquest ritme intern natural.

Behagligt, på något sätt

Vi kallar miljöer som människor bygger som svar på naturen för "skapade av människohand". Det som är skapat av människan ska vara bekvämt, men när material som plast och betong – som gör ett stort ingrepp i naturen – får dominera, börjar människor istället längta ut i naturen. Lämnar vi däremot naturen helt i fred dröjer det inte länge förrän marken täcks av damm och döda löv och växtligheten breder ut sig ohämmat. Det är nog därför som människor genom tiderna till viss del har accepterat naturen och till viss del hållit den i schack. Så, när du skapar ett boende eller en trädgård är det smaklöst att låta det som skapats av människohand att dominera. Vi måste låta naturen få ett visst spelrum och inte kratta upp vartenda löv eller beskära grönskan för mycket. Hemligheten med städning och att hålla ordning kanske ligger i det lagom behagliga: platser där naturen och det människan skapat möts och i all stillhet för en kamp mot varandra, som i vattenbrynet där vågorna bryts och sköljer in över sanden. Under 2019 åkte vi runt jorden och fotograferade scener där folk avbildades när de städade. Detta var innan covid-19 svepte fram över världen. Vi har undrat om människans innersta väsen ligger slumrande i den vanliga vardagsstädningen, som överskrider både kultur och samhälle. När hela världen hade stannat, fick dessa bilder och videoklipp oss att sakna våra vanliga rutiner. Oavsett hur tekniken utvecklas i framtiden så är vi människor alltid levande varelser, vi omfamnar en livsrytm som ständigt resonerar med kroppens inre djup. Vi kan röra oss framåt genom att uppmärksamma denna naturliga, inre rytm.

Delvist behageligt

Miljøer er skabt af mennesket som en reaktion på naturen. Dette kalder vi menneskeskabt. Når vi omgives med for mange kunstige materialer som plast og beton, begynder vi at længes efter naturlige aspekter. Hvis naturen overlades helt til sig selv, vil planter vokse vildt. Det er derfor, at mennesket igennem tiden har lært at acceptere og samarbejde med naturen. For at opretholde en balance mellem det menneskeskabte og naturen, er det vigtigt at de menneskeskabte produkter ikke tager overhånd. Det skal bruges med eftertanke og måde. Vi skal lade naturen udvikle sig, uden at indvolvere os for meget. Måske er hemmeligheden bag denne balance vedligeholdelse af vores jord. Det handler om at finde en moderat komfort på steder, hvor naturen og det menneskeskabte støder mod hinanden – ved vandkanterne, hvor havets bølger skyller op og vasker sandstrandene rene.

I 2019 rejste MUJI jorden rundt for at fotografere mennesker i færd med vedligeholdelse af jorden. Det var før, COVID-19 ramte os. Vi har nu overvejet, om indbegrebet af menneskets eksistens og værdier ligger i hverdagens almindelige vedlige-holdelsesprocesser, og dermed at passe på kloden og dets ressourcer. Da verden var gået i stå, mindede disse billeder og videoer os om vores gamle hverdagsrutiner.

Uanset hvor meget teknologien vil udvikle sig i fremtiden, er mennesket et rutinepræget væsen. Mennesket vil derfor altid foretrække en tryg livsrytme, der bestandigt giver genklang i kroppens indre. Vi kan komme videre og udvikle os, hvis vi lytter til denne naturlige rytme i både mennesket og naturen.

Sopivan mukavaa

Kutsumme ihmisten luonnosta muokkaamia ympäristöjä "ihmisen tekemiksi". Ihmisen tekemän tulisi olla mukavaa, mutta kun materiaalit, kuten muovi ja betoni, jotka tunkeutuvat luontoon tai kuluttavat sitä, leviävät laajalle, ihminen alkaa kaivata luontoa. Ja toisaalta, jos jätämme luonnon täysin rauhaan, pöly ja pudonneet lehdet kertyvät ja kasvit rehottavat villisti. Tämän seurauksena ihmiset ovat historian saatossa alkaneet elää hyväksyen luonnon oman olemuksen tiettyyn pisteeseen saakka ja muokaten sitä hillitysti. Niinpä asuintalosta tai puutarhasta tulee epämiellyttävä ja mauton, jos sen ulkomuodosta tehdään liian dominoiva. Meidän tulee antaa luonnon olla kohtuullisesti valloillaan, emme saa haravoida liikaa pudonneita lehtiä emmekä katkoa ja saksia liikaa luonnon vehreyttä. Aivan kuten rannalla, missä aallot huuhtelevat hiekkaa, puhdistamisen salaisuus on siinä, missä ihmisen toiminta ja luonto kohtaavat toisensa - ihmisten tavoitellessa "sopivaa mukavuutta". Vuonna 2019 kuljimme ympäri maailman valokuvaamassa ihmisiä erilaisissa puhdistamistilanteissa. Tämä oli ennen kuin COVID-19 tuli maailmaan. Mietimme, uinuuko ihmisyyden syvin olemus päivittäisessä ja tavallisessa, kulttuurin ja sivilisaation rajat ylittävässä puhdistamistyössä. Kun koko maailma on pysähtyi, nämä kuvat ja videot saivat meidät kaipaamaan omia rutiinejamme. Edistyipä teknologia tulevaisuudessa miten pitkälle tahansa, ihmiset ovat eläviä olentoja, joiden elämän perusolemukseen kuuluu syvälle kehoon resonoiva rytmi. Mennään eteenpäin huomioiden tämä luonnollinen, sisäinen rytmi.

Dễ chịu, theo cách nào đó

Chúng tôi gọi môi trường mà con người đã tạo ra để ứng phó với thiên nhiên là "nhân tạo". Nhân tạo thì luôn tiện lợi nhưng khi các vật liệu ăn mòn và tàn phá thiên nhiên như nhựa và bê tông lan tràn khắp nơi, con người bắt đầu khao khát thiên nhiên. Tuy nhiên, nếu cứ mặc cho thiên nhiên như vậy, đất bụi và lá rụng sẽ chất đống và cây cối sẽ phát triển ngoài kiểm soát. Vì thế, về mặt lịch sử, con người đã sinh sống bằng cách chấp nhận thiên nhiên ở mức độ nào đó và có thể kiểm soát một cách ôn hòa. Và do vậy, khi tạo một nơi cư ngụ hoặc một khu vườn, thật là khiếm nhã và vô vị nếu để yếu tố nhân tạo nổi trội. Chúng ta phải cho phép thiên nhiên ngự trị ở mức độ vừa phải, đừng quét sạch lá rụng hoặc tỉa tót cây quá mức. Giống như ở bờ biển, nơi những con sóng vỡ làm sạch bãi cát, bí mật của việc làm sạch có thể tìm thấy ở nơi mà sự can dự của con người và thiên nhiên chống chọi lẫn nhau, để theo đuổi "sự thoải mái vừa phải" của chúng ta.

Năm 2019, chúng tôi đi vòng quanh thế giới và ghi lại hình ảnh con người đang dọn dẹp. Sự kiện này xảy ra trước khi COVID-19 lan tràn khắp thế giới. Chúng tôi đã tự hỏi liệu bản chất của con người có nằm im lìm trong công việc dọn dẹp hàng ngày và thông thường vượt lên trên văn hóa và văn minh không. Ngày nay, khi cả thế giới dừng lại, những bức ảnh và video này làm cho chúng tôi nhớ về những thói quen thông thường của mình. Cho dù công nghệ có tiến bộ như thế nào trong tương lai, con người vẫn là những sinh vật sống, ôm lấy nhịp sống luôn cộng hưởng với từng thở thịt của chúng ta. Chúng ta có thể tiến bước theo nhịp điệu tự nhiên này.

เหตุผลของความสบายใจ

เราเรียกสภาพแวดล้อมที่มนุษย์สร้างขึ้นเพื่อตอบสนองต่อธรรมชาติว่า "สิ่งที่มนุษย์สร้างขึ้น" ทั้งนี้แม้ว่าสิ่งที่มนุษย์สร้างขึ้นนั้นควรจะให้ความสะดวกสบาย แต่เมื่อมีการใช้วัสดุที่กัดกร่อนหรือกลืนกินธรรมชาติอย่างพลาสติกและคอนกรีตกันอย่างแพร่หลาย ผู้คนก็จะเริ่มหันกลับมานึกถึงธรรมชาติ แม้กระนั้นหากเราปล่อยให้ธรรมชาติเป็นไปตามครรลองเพียงอย่างเดียว ก็จะกลายเป็นว่ามีฝุ่นผงและใบไม้ร่วงกองหนารวมถึงพืชพรรณต่างๆ งอกเงยซอกซอนไปทุกแห่งหน และด้วยเหตุนี้จากอดีตที่ผ่านมา มนุษย์จึงดำรงชีวิตด้วยการยอมรับธรรมชาติในระดับหนึ่ง ควบคู่ไปกับการควบคุมธรรมชาติให้อยู่ในระดับที่พอดี แม้แต่การสร้างบ้านหรือสวน หากมีสิ่งที่มนุษย์สร้างขึ้นอยู่มากเกินไป ก็ดูแปลกประหลาดและไร้รสนิยม เราจึงต้องปล่อยให้ธรรมชาติเป็นไปตามครรลองบ้าง เช่น การไม่กวาดใบไม้ที่ร่วงลงมาจนเกลี้ยง หรือเลือกที่จะไม่ทำการตัดหญ้าออกจนหมด บางทีความลับสุดยอดของการทำความสะอาดอาจค้นพบได้ในสถานที่ที่ธรรมชาติกับสิ่งที่มนุษย์สร้างขึ้นอยู่เคียงข้างกัน เช่น บริเวณริมฝั่งน้ำที่มีคลื่นซัดหาดทราย และนั่นคือการค้นหา "ความสะดวกสบายในระดับกำลังดี" ของเรา

ในปี 2019 เราได้ออกเดินทางไปทั่วโลกเพื่อเก็บภาพผู้คนกับการทำความสะอาด ซึ่งเป็นช่วงก่อนที่จะเกิดการแพร่ระบาดของโรคโควิด-19 เราสงสัยมาตลอดว่าแก่นแท้ของมนุษย์นั้นแท้จริงแล้วอาจซ่อนตัวอยู่เงียบๆ ท่ามกลางกิจวัตรการทำความสะอาดที่ทำอยู่เป็นประจำทุกวัน ซึ่งอาจเป็นสิ่งที่อยู่เหนือกว่าวัฒนธรรมและอารยธรรมก็เป็นได้ ณ เวลานี้ที่ทั้งโลกต่างหยุดนิ่ง ภาพถ่ายและวิดีโอเหล่านี้ทำให้เราหวนรำลึกถึงกิจวัตรที่เคยทำเป็นปกติ ไม่ว่าเทคโนโลยีในอนาคตจะก้าวหน้าเพียงใด แต่มนุษย์ก็ยังคงเป็นสิ่งมีชีวิตที่ครอบงำจังหวะแห่งชีวิตซึ่งยังคงก้องกังวานอยู่ในส่วนลึกของตัวเราอยู่เสมอ และเราจะก้าวต่อไปข้างหน้าได้หากหันมาสนใจจังหวะแห่งธรรมชาติดังกล่าวที่แอบซ่อนตัวอยู่ภายใน

السعادة، دون تكلف

تُعرف البيئة المحيطة التي قام الإنسان بإنشائها للتكيف والتعايش مع الطبيعة بـ "البيئة التي صنعها الإنسان" والتي يُفترض أن تكون مريحة وتتماشى مع أسلوب ومتطلبات الحياة، ولكن عندما تبدأ المواد الصناعية التي يستخدمها الإنسان بكثرة مثل البلاستيك والإسمنت بالتعدي على الطبيعة أو تسبب لها الأضرار، يبدأ الإنسان بالحنين والاشتياق للطبيعة البسيطة. ولكن إذا تركنا الطبيعة دون عناية، سوف تتجمع الأتربة وتتراكم أوراق الشجر المتساقطة وتنمو النباتات بشكل خارج عن السيطرة. على مر الزمان، عاش الإنسان في رحاب الطبيعة بانسجام مقبول إلى حد ما مع المحافظة عليها دون مبالغة بالعناية أو إهمال. ولذلك، إذا قام الإنسان ببناء منزل أو أنشأ حديقة، فمن غير اللائق أن تتسبب أعماله بالتعدي على الطبيعة. يتوجب علينا أحياناً أن نسمح بسيطرة الطبيعة إلى حد ما. فكما تعمل الأمواج المتكسرة على تنظيف الشواطئ والرمال، يسعى الإنسان للتوازن مع الطبيعة للتوصل إلى مفهوم "حياة مريحة ولكن معتدلة وموازنة مع الطبيعة".

في العام 2019، سافرنا حول العالم لنقوم بالتقاط صور لشعوب مختلفة أثناء قيامهم بأعمال التنظيف قبل أن يجتاح فيروس كوفيد-19 العالم. لقد كانت رؤيتنا تتمحور حول ما يقوم به الإنسان من أعمال يومية إعتيادية للعناية بالنظافة لترتقي بالثقافة والحضارة. واليوم، بينما يتوقف العالم عن الحركة نسبياً، نفتقد الروتين اليومي المعتاد عند مطالعة تلك الصور ومقاطع الفيديو. ومهما تطورت التكنولوجيا في المستقبل، فإن الإنسان قد اعتاد على نمط حياة يتوافق مع أسلوبه، وعليه فأنه يمكننا التقدم مع احترام هذا الأسلوب والإيقاع الداخلي.

Photography coordination

Nippon Design Center, Inc.
FLORA JASMINE
DOKUWA COMMUNICATIONS
I Love Paper bag co.,Ltd.
北京和创图文制作有限公司

Permission

CLEANING

CLEANING

CLEANING

Concept and art direction	Kenya Hara
Editing and design	Kenya Hara, Takuya Seki
Photography	Yoshihiko Ueda (pp.158–167, 208–209, 212–213)
	Taiki Fukao (except as noted above)
Text	Kenya Hara, Takuya Seki, Mariko Hara
English translation	Maggie Kinser Hohle, Yukiko Naito
Illustration	Yukiyo Nemoto, Megumi Ohno, Haruna Furusato
Producer	Satoshi Muraki
Printing and Binding	Belvédère Art Books, Oosterbeek, the Netherlands
Publishing	Lars Müller Publishers GmbH
	Zurich, Switzerland
	www.lars-mueller-publishers.com
	(First published 2020 by Ryohin Keikaku Co.,Ltd.)

ISBN 978-3-03778-732-8

Distributed in North America, Latin America, Caribbean
by ARTBOOK I D.A.P
www.artbook.com

Printed in the Netherlands

Project by